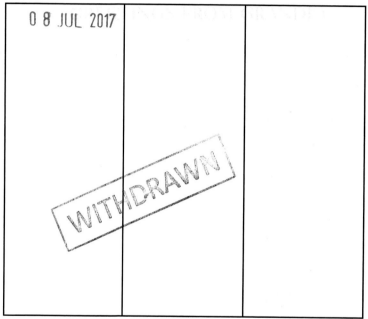

Jack Mapanje is a poet, linguist, editor and human rights activist. He received the 1988 Rotterdam Poetry International Award for his first book of poems, *Of Chameleons and Gods* (1981) and the USA's Fonlon-Nichols Award for his contribution to poetry and human rights. He was head of the Department of English at the University of Malawi where the Malawi authorities arrested him in 1987 after his first book of poems had been banned, and he was released in 1991 after spending three years, seven months and sixteen days in prison, following an international outcry against his incarceration.

He has since published five poetry books, *The Chattering Wagtails of Mikuyu Prison* (1993) from Heinemann, and *Skipping Without Ropes* (1998), *The Last of the Sweet Bananas: New & Selected Poems* (2004), *Beasts of Nalunga* (2007) and *Greetings from Grandpa* (2016) from Bloodaxe, as well as his prison memoir, *And Crocodiles Are Hungry at Night* (Ayebia Clarke Publishing, 2011); he co-edited three anthologies, *Oral Poetry from Africa* (1983), *Summer Fires: New Poetry of Africa* (1983) and *The African Writers' Handbook* (1999); and edited the acclaimed *Gathering Seaweed: African Prison Writing* (2002). *Beasts of Nalunga* was shortlisted for the Forward Prize for Best Collection in 2007.

Mapanje has held residences in the Netherlands, the Republic of Ireland and throughout Britain, including two years with the Wordsworth Trust at Dove Cottage in Cumbria. He lives in exile in York with his family, and is a visiting professor in the faculty of art at York St John University. He was awarded an honorary doctorate by the University of Bedfordshire in 2015.

Jack Mapanje

GREETINGS
FROM GRANDPA

BLOODAXE BOOKS

ISBN: 978 1 78037 311 9

First published 2016 by
Bloodaxe Books Ltd,
Eastburn,
South Park,
Hexham,
Northumberland NE46 1BS.

www.bloodaxebooks.com
For further information about Bloodaxe titles
please visit our website or write to
the above address for a catalogue.

Supported using public funding by
**ARTS COUNCIL
ENGLAND**

Cover design: Neil Astley & Pamela Robertson-Pearce.

Printed in Great Britain by Bell & Bain Limited, Glasgow, Scotland, on
acid-free paper sourced from mills with FSC chain of custody certification.

*To adorable grand children
and their parents for calming
the nerves and fears of exile*

ACKNOWLEDGEMENTS

Grateful thanks to Alison Rigg, colleagues and students in the Faculty of Arts, York St John University; Julian Forrester and Polly Clark at Cove Park writers' retreat, Scotland, where 'Kalikalanje' was structured; Professor Arua eke Arua, Tiro Sebina, Barolong Seboni, David Kerr and other colleagues and students in the Department of English, Faculty of Humanities, University of Botswana, where the first version of this selection was assembled when I was on sabbatical leave among them; Physics Professor Pearson Luhanga for printing the original drafts of the poems at home without tiring; and to Jack Little in Mexico.

Earlier versions of some of these poems have appeared online, in books, pamphlets, newspapers, poetry magazines including, recently, *POEM*, *Poetry Wales, Modern Poetry in Translation* (*MPT*) in the UK, and others in France, Germany, Mexico, Malawi, Uganda and Botswana; many thanks to the editors who accepted them.

For compiling this final version with a peaceful mind, I gratefully acknowledge the financial assistance of Eileen Gunn and her executive committee at the Royal Literary Fund, London and a grant from Paula Johnson and her committee at the Society of Authors, the Authors' Foundation and K. Blundell Trust, London. Special hugs to Neil Astley and his diligent team at Bloodaxe Books for the fine production of this definitive edition.

CONTENTS

Exile is round in shape:
a circle, a ring.

PABLO NERUDA

Imagining Home

If they should ask how
you lasted for so long
wandering in alien lands
after your country of
birth had spewed you
out of her belly, if they
should wonder at your
narratives crafted out-
side landscapes of home,
if town or village chiefs
should demand *chambo*
from their son's fishing
tackle or offal from his
game hunt, if anyone
should ever ask, tell them
true truths: in the land
of the free the lakes are
cold, there are no hippos,
no crocodiles, few rabbits
race up the craggy hills;
you were a mere tenant
on the tobacco farms of
invisible global despots:
they reap most from their
toil those who bend back-
wards the furthest; but
you were delighted for
the shelter, for genuine
friendships too, though
often you still pined for
the purple jacarandas,
the dry earthy dust of
home, where you hoped
to return wholesome one
day – doesn't chameleon

wear the colours of his
adopted twigs, doesn't
snake crawl back to his
pit of origin, eventually?

Surviving Freedom in Sunderland

And should the traffic police disrupt
your direct route from A19 because
another truck has shed its load in front
of you; should your diverted traffic
snail tediously past toughened faces
of villages struggling to rescue their
dignity after long lost coal and ship-
building industries; should you lose
your way zigzagging, crisscrossing
the city's mazes: cul-de-sacs, one-way
streets, weird roundabouts and green,
grey, white, other bridges; should you
begin to panic about your delay and
the petrol running out –
                                    Do not frighten
the senior citizens unravelling the lyrics
of their seagulls flying over the seafront
nor interrupt the Empire Theatre box
office girls forever chattering online;
just take on the city's three old ladies
at the nearby bus stop, they'll show you
the Green Terrace Campus, precisely
where your audience is waiting to hear,
gratis, how you survive your freedom.

Lu's Home Delivery (Welwyn Garden City)

Lu swore that babies born at home was
not her kind of thing; she'd have her next
born in hospital like her first, Nathan;
it was always safe there among doctors,
midwives, paramedics and all, and her
Stephen would be around to hold her hand;
but when Lu rang the hospital that her
baby was due and coming, the midwife
and her paramedics thought the better
of it and insisted, without first checking
on the mother, Lu's time could not be nigh;
she must take more paracetamol until
the water had truly broken and the baby
actually there, when she could ring again,
if she liked. Then Lu's visiting mum,
a radiant midwife once and knew her
daughter better, told Stephen to get the car
ready for hospital; but before Lu reached
the door from upstairs, mum frantically
yelled for whatever gloves were available –
with Stephen's help their baby screamed
to life at the door – the old midwife did
what she had to do. When the ambulance,
paramedics and midwife finally arrived,
Lu's baby boy was peacefully shoaled. 'Well
done you!' they barked at Lu, Stephen,
the baby and their midwife; after cutting
the cord and pretending to do whatever
else was left undone, they returned to base
without shame or apology – that was when
the baby's real midwife rang York at 3 a.m. –
I gather Stephen and Lu did not bother
to sue the hospital for negligence; they
simply christened their son Ethan Lumuli
to bind him to his familial habit for 'light!'

12

The Carwash, Clifton Moor, York

When Mukisa shelved his post
as assistant chef at the students

cafeteria on Chirunga campus, he
told us and his mum up country

he was flying to Nairobi for an
advanced course in catering; five

years later, he walked into my
Leeds University office anxious

about the protests and riots for
multiparty politics back home;

stammering as he recounted how
he'd managed to enter Leeds for

a PhD degree in catering, after
Nairobi, he said he often became

a night cabby to survive; I stayed
put and recalled his lucrative career

as a young pioneer recruit nailing
his president's political rebels from

Nairobi, London, Toronto and other
world cities. But fifteen years on

yesterday, did I not chance upon
Mukisa at Tesco's car park: could

he wash and wax my filthy car;
his price was the most competitive

in town, he avowed. I took him on,
then asked what had become of his

gainful task as a night cabby hunting
his leader's enemies with his Leeds

PhD degree in catering; he gazed
at me past his goggles, kicked his

bucket, and fixed my car with his
Polish mates fretting beside him.

Princess Alexandra Smiling (Luxembourg)

After driving on the right for the first
time, the strains die down. We scratch
for the second name for Judy's baby-
girl as we re-enter Dr Bohler's clinic,
to give mum and baby another cheer;
prophet brothers Joseph and Daniel are
still bubbly that the name they chose for
their sister, when daddy first said mum's
going to have a baby, has been accepted
by Uncle Lika's entire family; only daddy's
absence perplexes the boys: why should
we mark Alexandra's coming without
daddy, why did he prefer reunion with
his Uganda clan now, is the grandma in
Masaka not well, perhaps? Daddy will
have to explain. At our raucous re-entry
in Dr Bohler's ward, however, Princess
Alexandra opens her large brown eyes,
smiles a glorious smile. We are bowled
over with wonder and joy at her 'Masaka
nose' and 'Masaka smile' – our London
aches fighting for urgent Luxembourg
Schengen visas are rewarded. We text
our ecstasy to daddy and clan; they text
back their thrill, offering Alexandra's
second name, Lisungu, the incumbent
grandma's. Driving back to Leudelange
Village that evening, the sky has dark
clouds scudding – 'an African deluge
in Luxembourg,' grandma prophesies.
The universe flashes thrice, thunderbolt
growls, hailstones pelt the windscreen,
we wipe snowflakes that float like kapok,
aimless. After totalling all Europe's seasons
in one day, Daniel recalls Alexandra's

nose and smile, the vehicle reverberates
with bellyfuls of giggle. 'Grandpa, will
you write a tiny poem for Alexandra, I'll
read it to her!' Joseph boasts, advising:
'Press the top knob to open the garage!'
So, smug in the sofa, we sing of Alexandra's
arrival and the scary drive on the right.

Some Anglo-Deutsch-Malawi Wedding!
(for Dambu & Ulf)

The battle for the German Schengen visas
finally won, after appeals and other pains,
we begin with the famed Wartburg Castle.

Passing through the archway, clusters of
flying doves greet us. We watch them settle
above the 'Luther Room', which we find

musty, its desk, chair still defiant, husky:
Martin Luther assembled his bearings here;
for ten months, he shielded his neck from his

Pope's smoking guillotines, changing world
history forever, as he first translated the Bible
into the German. But let's drive to Eisenach

for Kaka and I to sample the city's beer at
Bach's Bier Garden as the rest of the wedding
party explores the markets and shops before

we set off for the pre-wedding *Polterabend*
ritual at Steinbach Shooting Club. Here,
as the party marks each porcelain smashed

with shouts and cheers, we will mill around
glowing fires, mouths watering for the barbecue
sausages sizzling, the smooth German beer,

the smoky wine, hoping the shards can truly
bring our Dambu and Ulf the good luck that
this custom insists upon. And when the Afro-

Deutsch disco starts, may the wedding crowd
not dance the night into dawn; for tomorrow,
the couple, dressed to kill, need their stamina

walking cavalcades of singing, chanting, dancing
aficionados from the Kulturhotel Kaiserhof
to Standesamt, where they'll emerge 'husband

and wife' amid more cheer, song, dance until
they reach the front of the Standesamt. There,
the groom this side and bride the other will

seesaw their 'Wedding Log' till pieces drop.
And still clutching at their pieces, they'll open
the birdcage beside them, release six doves

to the wild – their entry into the world will
have been effected to extended applause and
dance from fans and bemused onlookers non-

plussed by the free champagne chanced upon.
Then the wedding party will move to official
venue, the Kulturhotel Kaiserhof where, after

the rituals of wedding-cake-cutting, bride
feeding cake to groom's parents and groom
feeding cake to bride's parents, sumptuous

dinner threatens, to be strewn by delightful
if winding speeches, jibes, jokes that will lure
us to another prolonged after dinner dance

speckled by more bountiful German beer, wine.
When the stretched surprise dawn fireworks
grace another hectic day, let the jolly staff at

Kulturhotel Kaiserhof shriek: 'When will we
enjoy another brilliantly rowdy but cheerful
Anglo-Deutsch-Malawi wedding carnival?'

Watching Palestinians Being Butchered

After the gorgeous festival of Anglo-Deutsch-
Malawi wedding at Kulturhotel Kaiserhof,
why must we now confront Palestinians being
butchered in these senseless cyclic war games
where you warn your adversaries to vacate
their homes and shelters (you've effectively
surrounded with high concrete walls) so you
can bomb them more humanely; what kind
of war is this that must go on and on while
the rest of the world looks on, befuddled?
Günter Grass was certainly right 'to be sick of
the West's hypocrisy' and what must be said;
or was it the weary world powers, who carved
their favourite state hurriedly on Palestinian
land after their long drawn out wars, that are
inexcusably flawed? And when will we begin
to see that all walls must eventually crumble,
like Berlin Wall, what will it take to hope here?

The Three People I Met in Diaspora

I

I'll sing of the buffalo of a grandpa
that I knew in the diaspora once;
he drove more than ten thousand
miles every year, defying freezing
showers, muddy snows and subzero
temperatures; from the swamps of
Withernsea to the sands of Morecambe
Bay, from Shetland to Lewes and
globes in between; I watched the bull
swap one scrap heap of a car after
another, seven times in two decades;
I stalked him fume at inland-revenue
self-assessment forms he, apparently,
did not need filling out, but trip after
trip I saw him declare his paltry wages;
when the forms were sent back as he
perpetually ticked the wrong boxes,
the buffalo grated his teeth carping,
'I ain't done with you yet, who does
not need the extra bob to manage their
mortgage?' Asked why he did not fill
out the forms properly, why inland-
revenue officers fined him for sending
their forms late, the buffalo rumbled
his willing reply, 'That's the fun you
miss about diasporas dear, for these
forms do not listen – pretty much like
politicians everywhere!' Was I dead!

II

I'll sing of the sunflower of a grandma
that I provoked in the diaspora once;
she had dumped her perfect nursing

profession in Africa for sleepless nights
as carer in diaspora; when I challenged
her why, she curtly replied, 'The cock-
roaches back home took for granted
the sweat, blood, tears I shed throughout
my nursing career; frankly, I'd rather wipe
fat foreign bums than lose my dignity
to thankless beasts of home! This way
I could send to school more grand sons
and daughters.' Was I utterly crushed!

III

I'll sing of bush-tailed shrews of comrades
that I resist in the diaspora all the time;
only yesterday did one inflame me with:
'Why don't you go home to resolve your
"cash-gate" affair that has broken out there;
surely, you have the integrity, the gravitas
they need!' And when I said, 'But am just
another flea in diaspora unaware of ongoing
cash-gates; nor am I your ordinary pushover!'
comrade shrew merely whined and wept
at the humour that nourishes our diasporas.

Grandpa Travelling Again?

On the road again;
this time bound for
sands of the Sahara
to hunt wild kudu
where lions roam
among the gazelle;
indeed, twenty grey
years in one freezing
mire was a miracle;
and son, to become
a true tenant on this
global farm you call
home, do not botch it;
do not fear, do not fight,
above all do not mock
those vulture-beaked
men or the freckled
hunchback women
who block your way
draped in vipers on
your epic adventures;
wring every dewdrop
of their wisdom and
leave footprints not
lips there, as the sages
said, once upon a time.

Greetings from Grandpa

(for Joseph, Daniel, Nathan & Co)

You said I should write
you a teeny-weeny poem,
a poem that's easy to recite
to Alexandra and Ethan;
I am sending you a poem
that relates and leaps like
the pelican on Okavango
Delta, leaping from green
water lilies to brown floats,
a poem which springs like
the sly monkeys of Gaborone
screeching from tree branch
to rooftop, a poem which
rings bells day and night,
here, there, everywhere like
the lead-cows of The Village;
tomorrow I will send you
a wee poem which rumbles
like the lion or roars like
father-drums, a wee poem
that quivers and smokes
like the muscles of Batswana
dancers bouncing at their
brides' wedding jamboree.

The Three *Dikgosi* of Gaborone
(A history of Botswana by our guide)

'You tower heavenwards, three gods,
each polished in 2.5 tones of bronze
the winning North Korean sculptor
cast to your glistening memory; you
stand tall, poised, imperial; colonial
secretary Joseph Chamberlain and his
scheming pal Cecil Rhodes would have
looked minuscule, dwarfed beside you!
Borraetsho, it was not in vain that your
forebears won Ndebele's bloody Zulu
wars or fought off Jan Van Riebeeck
or overcame the Dutch East India Co.
and other deadly invaders; how could
you let Chamberlain and Rhodes win?
You prayed only that Reverend William
Charles Willoughby, Edwin Lloyd and
friends should not dither but take you
straight to the listening monarch. For,
despite Lord Chamberlain's manoeuvres,
you knew you would sway any British
public that let you speak on your people's
behalf; you had the rhetoric and charm
that would lure queens: 'We, the three
dikgosi, speaking for our people, would
rather die under Your Majesty's direct
shelter than cower under the servitude
of Cecil Rhodes' regime!' How devious
then of Lord Chamberlain, who knew
that the listening monarch would grant
your request, (offering you a bible each
besides!), how disingenuous of colonial
secretary Chamberlain thereafter to slur:
'It's utterly disgusting to be beaten by
the Nigers!' *Borraetsho*, our inspiration,
history, culture; the nation salutes you!'

The Rush for Independence Celebrations
(for David Kerr)

They are all gone to their
cattle posts, kraals, villages,
to celebrate independence
among real people; colleague
Maude even bragged about
visiting the golden beaches
of Cape Town instead on this
umpteenth anniversary of
her liberation; they are gone
leaving our shopping malls,
ATM holes in walls, churches
empty; they are gone taking
their money and morals with
them. Let us, therefore, you
and I they call *makwerekwere*,
with no cattle posts, no kraals
to boast about, let us, brother,
hope the ATMs they have left
behind can stock up quickly
for us to visit *Botswana Crafts*,
The Golf Club, Eros, wherever
live jazz guitars are twanging
and saxophones blustering; if
they too have joined the rush,
we'll race their naked streets,
stop for oxtail & pap at *Sanitas*
or some café that must open
on this anniversary of peace.

Load-shedding

This dark will go on forever
so stand up, feel your way
to the laptop desk where
the drawer has a box of matches,
strike one and enter the kitchen;
in the bottom drawer of the third
shelf are candles, light one,
take it to the living room,
sit down and ask your Dee why
she decided to feed the monkeys
that woke you up so early today
squealing, leaping from tree branch
to rooftop, as if you did not matter,
doesn't she know there are people
out there who would do with
a banana and an orange?

'But we are not out there
we are here in the dark, for another
three hours probably; and those
monkeys were sweet: one carefully
peeling the banana then nibbling at it,
the other first wrestling with
the orange pips like you and me;
we shared pawpaw with monkeys
at Ku Chawe Inn breakfast on Zomba
Plateau once, what of these? I would
do it again any day and when the lights
come back on I'll Skype Joseph
in Luxembourg or Nathan in
Welwyn Garden City about their
grandma's encounters with
the cute monkeys of Gaborone.'

First Lobatse International Beef Festival

When Barolong's verse refused to come, he
dreamt up another way of beating the muse;
with Lobatse still capital of the finest beef
in the land, he recalled the beer, wine, brandy,
whisky festivals he had known – the bud for
Lobatse beef carnival began to push. But we
understood the seminal seed to be Barolong's
subterranean dread of the painful global blood-
letting festivals of human carnage he could
not decrypt – the European, Arab, African,
Asian and other wars where father butchers
son butchers brother butchers uncle butchers
sister butchers this butchers that butchers
sometimes ta-ta-ta and boom! 'Allahu Akbar!'
Glory be, why doesn't someone for once think
Lobatse beef fest instead? So Barolong told
a friend to tell friends to tell clans of friends,
local plus overseas clients of Botswana beef,
to bring boxes of ice cubes with their choicest
whiskies, brandies, gins, wines, beers, softies
to Lobatse Town Park – that's why Tiro, Dee
and I drove there; and as Tiro wildly inveigled
every kid in sight to his creative writing project,
guys roamed the gardens, while others snug
in goatskin stools, camping chairs, blankets,
kept on talking, drinking, laughing, picking
delectable chunks of sirloin, rump, t-bone steaks
to braai here, there, everywhere; meanwhile
Barolong treated the tradition-inclined to top
tripe and offal, niftily fried at the *kgotla*, served
with basmati rice, or delicately cooked pap. So,
as dancers' rattles, body-and-head-gear shook
to the thump-clap rhythm of drums, feet and
hands at the park's mini stadium, as they leapt
in praise of their chiefs, before jazz guitars and

saxophones seized the arena, everybody kept on
braaing, chewing, arguing, drinking, laughing
into sunset – thanking God, *Badimo*, Barolong
for the first festival of the finest Lobatse beef!

Farewell to the Mopipi Tree

(for Tiro, Alec & Co)

Your farewell messages and signatures
inscribed on Margaret Taylor's postcard
of the mopipi tree I madly drove across
the land to prize are overwhelming: *We're*
missing you already; life's not the same;
best wishes for the future; what a blessing
to have had you; why did we let you go so...
But Taylor's mopipi tree with her khaki-
brown scrub, ash-green acacias against
the grey canvas, purple-bronze sinews of
dead roots on arthritic trunk and branches –
Margaret Taylor's mopipi tree does not get
there; I'd rather the candid mopipi tree of
Gaborone Main Shopping Mall, flouting
the heat-waves as blackbirds, swallows,
finches flutter among the branches while
the pigeons coo, lizards and squirrels dash
about their diamond lines; I prefer pretty
honest Mochudi girls dislodging plastic
tables under their mopipi tree, unrolling
hand-woven cloths and, placing their juicy
oranges, tangerines, pineapples, mangoes
challenging: *Buy me six, so I too can enter*
college next year, here are sweets for kids
at home! Tiro, must I return for the writing
surgeries with the kids at the city museum?

The Note (On Returning Home)

This is it, she said, pointing at
the mound with the Bible she
had brought from the house,
this is where we buried your
brother, and it's not the shock
of thieves stealing the wreaths
we heaped on his mound only
to sell them again to their next
bereaved client which bothered
me, that's norm today; it's my

discovering two months before
your visit what had troubled
my dearest man the last years
of our lives together. And why
didn't I open these pages before
his passing? She strikes her chest
beads of tears running down her
cheeks, then pulls out the note:
this is what's been wrenching
my heart since I unearthed it –

Darling, you said I tormented
you when I turned the other side
each time you joked about yearning
for another kid! I am sorry, but I
did not know how to tell you: one
infidelity gave me the incurable
curse I did not wish to pass on; I
love you and the children, dearly;
you'll always be my finest angels;
forgive me & pray when I am gone.

He'd placed that note between
the leaves of St Paul's letter to
the Romans we often discussed,
she says, he knew I'd find it in
the end, just that it took forever.
I wipe my teardrops which fell on
the pages that had kept their note,
scoop dust with my bare hands and
fling it at our garlands; leading her
to the car, we drive back, silent.

Crossing Linthipe Bridge II

As you crossed Linthipe
Bridge all those years ago,
the spectacle of tenants
labouring on both sides of
the road cautioned you to
drive carefully, for men
women, youths, families
were crossing – planting,
weeding, harvesting their
president's crop of tobacco
or his clique's; battalions
of beetles pushed wheel-
barrows of seedling, leaf,
fertiliser, dodging green
tractors (bought with funds
freed from the accountant
general's drawers); you saw
sweat and tears gleaming
on tense muscles and knew
the sneezing, the coughing,
the chest heaving, as hands
hung stall upon stall of fire-
cured barley or sun-dried
tobacco, stashing the finest
leaf for city auction floors
to recoup millions for their
masters, pittance for their
toil! But crossing Linthipe
Bridge today weed, grass,
bush choke the farms you
once feared; you can only
guess at the scorpions, snakes
foxes, the myriad monsters
that guard the derelict sheds,
shacks, barns, as bemused

passengers openly whisper:
have accountant general's
coffers dried up then, won't
the tenants return to share
out the farms, or the chiefs
to reclaim the land they were
bullied into selling cheaply
to the fallacious politicians,
won't the current masters of
the political arena, already
redesigning your lives upon
dead despot's dated dogmas
with their bogus ethnicities,
won't they blot you out with
another brutal barren brush?
As your rattling bus veers
right overtaking exhausted
queues of vehicles waiting
on empty fuel tanks, your
heart weeps for these cities
subjected to endemic road
cracks, potholes, water and
power-cuts; nor do your ripe
papayas, the sweet potatoes,
mangoes in season that you
buy through windows offer
clues for the revolt looming –
if nothing worse reproaches
your desperate state sooner.

Balamanja North Beach Revisited

(for Charles & Flora Kahumbe)

I know this sandy beach intimately
you could not walk this far nor fondle

the gentle ripples of this giant lake,
fifty miles across, lap-lapping at your

feet, as the Saturday breeze cools your
hangover and placates the fatigue of

another hectic drive across the country.
It was here Balamanja village women

called their chiefs traitors for selling
this beach to South African tourists

and other voyagers who, in the name of
tourism those years ago, built cottages

that zoned the village off their newly
acquired property. But when the new

owners began to invite more sojourners
free at their 'native-protected' homes,

avoiding the official hotels, even after
the sun had spun its new political life,

an irate district governor, seeking more
eloquent tourism, urged Charles, Flora

and other better-off local Shire high-
landers to liberate the beaches. Today

home grown tycoons are building lodges
and hotels yonder; Charles, Flora & sons

are into fishing big time; Balamanja
village can bathe, wash, draw its sand-

filtered water as of old; you and I can
surely stroll along the beach, kicking

little sand dunes, cork floats or picking
pebbles, beach shells, the odd baobab

fruit. I gather this baobab tree, recently
felled by gales, will be chopped and split –

firewood for all – do you feel the waves
of this vast lake throb with fresh verve?

Our Anthology of Martyrs Thickens

I will sing a new song to my country
for my dear country of birth
is marching again
marching for freedom
which exiled us in the years gone by
marching against rampant corruption
that got us jailed for pointing out
marching against *tribalism*
that someone is reinventing
marching unarmed for justice
marching unarmed for freedom
marching unarmed for peace
seeking unarmed the truth

I will sing a new song to my country
for my dear country of birth
is protesting again
protesting for fuel pumps gone dry;
protesting for sporadic cuts
of power and pipe-water –
where half the country is a mass of water!

I will sing a new song to my country
for my dear country of birth
is parading again
parading against chucking out
patrons who might just help
build bridges
or fill out yawning road cracks and potholes
or bring medicines in hospitals, clinics, villages,
or get books for schools;

I will sing a new song to my country
for my dear country of birth is mad
for letting foreign companies demand *forex*

from the reserve bank instead of bringing it in,
for letting men die at the uranium company
up north without asking why,
for letting Chinese builders come with their own
shovels, hoes, wheelbarrows, labour
to build *our* nation
instead of using local implements and people;

I will sing a new song to my country
for my dear country of birth has gone so bonkers
that mobile phones, blogs, Twitter, Facebooks
are challenging the expensive bugging
and tracking devices just purchased
to dare stop them talking
to exiles in diaspora
about how they could help fill
the tin-can lamps that have no paraffin,
imploring them to use money-grams
to sort out grain grinding mills
running out of diesel
in rural and urban markets;

I will sing a new song to my country
for my dear country of birth is
murdering its own people again without apology
leaving many maimed, wounded,
19 martyrs are already rested in Mzuzu,
student Robert Chasowa was left sprawling
cold on the campus cement in Blantyre,
university staff and students were tear-gassed
marching unarmed for justice
protesting unarmed for academic freedom
parading unarmed for peace
yelling unarmed for the truth.

But how many more people will be
murdered, how many left unburied
and for how long, Lord?

Oh, help me sing new songs for my country:
where did we go wrong
where did we buy this madness
where is the spirit that bonded us once
where are we coming from
where are we going?

On His Divine Reprieve: A Confession

Dear Lord, I am on my bended knees.
I am sorry I doubted your power
to intervene in human affairs, for
I had sung so many songs of pain
for my country's freedom, justice,
peace without getting the desired
result as I thought; I am very sorry I
dared You to wipe out our personal,
communal, national tears after years
of singing, dancing, crying for liberty,
justice, peace; I am so sorry, it just
felt like we had been weeping from
the wrong scripts as we could not
crack Your conundrum amid the noisy,
chaotic, muffled voices of our vociferous
generation; I am truly sorry. But did
we imagine one ordinary day waking
up to the shock of Herod, swaggering
on his throne, robed in gold, then struck
by Your angel! And Lord, how they
lied about him still alive and kicking,
what relief when the plot to revive him
in South Africa flunked, what culture
of hope suddenly descended at the
prospect of a woman – Herod's own
flinching foe – leading! Dear comrades
in academy and litigation, do not let
another Herod enter the arena; continue
to float this raft until it moors on the
shoreline of liberty, justice, peace – let's
sing glory to God's divine reprieve!

Considering Our Golden Jubilees

What verse shall I chant truly
to celebrate my country at fifty

what icon could words chisel
when the powers that be have

sold our pithiest wood to their
foreign partners abroad, hiding

their harvest? What song shall I
sing when a weird deadly virus

is debilitating the comrades in
litigation who won't preside over

the 'cash-gate' affair against one
of their own as they drank from

the same goblet once? What tune
should I hum after your battling

with punitive batons, teargas, clad
in red T-shirts, red ties, red scarfs,

shoving and kicking for academic
freedom, peace, justice? What chorus

can anyone marshal to guide today's
tender actors? I gravely despair.

*

Yet why must I throw the white
cockerel in the arena in defeat

when the enemy's well beaten?
I watched Idi Amin in a London

documentary taunt his aides to
a swimming contest once; no one

moved to outshine their chief's
clumsy splashes, for, memories

unfurled, memories of the open
graves for his innocent rebels, of

coffins scooped out, bullet-holed
skulls, machete-slit bones, other

scam strewn here, there, surging
hideously like cork floats washed

up the beaches of Lake Victoria –
but of course Idi Amin Dada won

the contest! So, what canticle, what
script will truly capture our jubilees?

The White Elephants of Home

(for Fiona & Co)

The white elephants these tyrants
bequeath us are truly corrupting:

names embossed on our bridges,
highways, hospitals, airports; red

brick buildings of their ill-conceived
self-named faculties; effigies, clan

feuds and other melancholia that
their regimes exact on the ordinary –

the white elephants despots leave
behind for us mortals are unsettling;

take our Chikangawa Forest, who
stripped to stumps that sweetheart

of the nation and sold its wood to
our new buddies – Asia, China or

whoever helped pocket the proceeds
their foxes buried in nooks far away?

As for those puzzling sacks upon
sacks of US dollars you uncovered

at state house after Herod's passing,
where did the rodents you beguiled

with praise songs, for them to keep
your health tight, acquire the avarice

to syphon shameless billions, build
their mansions or bribe your votes

to sneak another comrade rat into
power? And how far back do these

pilfering chains go that no spider's
web or wit will ever bait? So, when

you warn about bare-faced butterflies
snuffing our uranium today as ivory,

gold, diamonds deplete, it's the white
elephants our despots will bequeath

us that I dread, it's the tears running
down Mum's soft cheeks that I fear.

When Egypt Went Up in Flames

(A Letter to Mike Polela, Malawi)

My dear Mike, I returned home
safely, though dug in my chair
the box greeted me with virtual
Egypt going up in flames; it was
not the Cairo or Tahrir Square
we'd hoped we'd visit some day,
but thousands of youths, mostly
students, with banners, placards,
flames chanting: *Mubarak must go;*
we've had enough of his thirty-year
reign of terror! I rubbed my chin,
poured myself another glass of
Jameson 12 then flicked to other
channels only to see more Egypt
in flames. I recalled our chat on
Tunisia, where the Arab Spring
Revolution began; how the despot
there had vacated his farms at
the behest of hollering tenants;
you foresaw the demise for future
despots in our worldwide web
as I began to grasp the message
of Egyptian poets over the years
and Nawal El Saadawi's prose I
had taught from to typify the pain
Cairo, Suez, Alexandria and other
cities beyond had tussled for years.

But my heart waned: how long
would the flames last, how far
the revolution's tentacles; could
telegrams, telephones, faxes, web-
sites, blogs, Facebooks, YouTubes,
Twitter, whatever latest gadgetry –

rightly secure Egypt's liberty so
far so elusive? No matter. Dear
comrades in liberation struggle,
I see you, hear you and marvel
at your fuming flames of Egypt,
but your casualties frighten me:
not just the protesters fallen or
falling, or the political prisoners
you'll have to liberate, the new
constitution you'll have to map
out, women's dignity you'll have
to repair, above all, the military
you'll have to confine to barracks
to shield cycles of future dissent;
what terrify most are the echoes
across the borders where Egypt
is their cultural, political, social
hub; even from this self-deluding
lighthouse here, your Egypt in
flames will jolt, perhaps stagger
fans of Israel, Palestine, Arab Oil –
must I refill my glass then, should
I tap my foot and groove to your
Egypt in flames, won't your army
bounce back with more curfews?
Whatever, my warmest regards!

This TV Death So Mean: Libya

The death of a despot need not be
so dramatic, callous and gruesome,
whether or not he murdered more
tenants than rabid dogs on his farms;
whatever your take on truth and
reconciliation or vengeance that
belongs to the Lord, you could not
redress adequately the traumas that
the tenants wrestle under despots –
the men, women, children hit squads
torture to death, electrocute, burn
alive or simply *disappear*.
　　　　And what is it about despots,
why are they so exasperating, why
do they often bring it on themselves,
why do they always claim we love them
when the world knows even family
loves for fear? And dear investigative
chums, did we really need to watch
the brute writhing, gasping, the spirit
squeezed out of his sewage-crushed
body? Why must the world be denied
another tale of global duplicity hushed
by the death of this dictator who will
not face international courts now and
what hope does a nation freed hold
when its liberators begin to dither?

Somaliland Rebuilding, Hargeysa: An Outsider's View

(for Jama & Ayan)

The ex-British protectorate of Somaliland,
No longer engaged in local feuds, wrangles
And civil wars with her southern neighbours
Way down Mogadishu, feuds and wars that

Turned dense *agal* huts with matted fences
To ruins, debris, shards, dust – Somalilanders
At home and from diasporas are reasserting
Their roots. They are re-forging Hargeysa into

A peaceful, well-fortified capital city, and on
Their own terms. With Hargeysa Civil War
Memorial in the center and the MiG fighter
Jet that razed buildings down rudely poised –

A reminder how it mortified the city but gave
The nation freedom – today stone is rebuilding
On stone, brick on brick, glass on plate glass.
Edna Adan Ismail has transformed her humble

Health clinic into the rarest Maternity Hospital
Training most progressive nurses and midwives
Who service the remotest Somaliland villages;
Sage 'Hadraawi' enthralls audiences with his

Hypnotic Somali poetic rhythms, images, symbols;
Then come the chirpy men who chew their khat
After business, laughing; the men in sandals
And white robes salaaming; the women decent

In sweeping saris; despite the world that takes
No notice, everyone in Hargeysa is jostling
For their patch of road, street, land: chickens,
Goats, sheep, camels, donkey-carts, minibuses

Taxis and the endless file of men and women
Beside market walkways with their basket
Cages full of wads of money chasing your US
Dollars – everybody is re-designing Hargeysa

To their hearts desire. And it's working, I say!
There's no load shedding. The guns guarding
Gates or doors that matter are for Al-Shabaab
Who won't get here again after their fateful

Suicide bombs many years ago. So, when you next
Visit Hargeysa, drive gently beside the sidewalks,
People are rebuilding there – it's a shame we do
Not often recognise little nations that function!

Saved from Comrade Hippo's Grace

(for Tupali & Co)

So, if you ever desire to become a man
son, do not row your canoe away from
other canoes, alone, on a crisp morning
drifting, to play the champ with hippo's
jaws – however gracious the beast. You
cannot avoid elephant's feet twice, they
say, nor should you expect another *Tupali*
to grab his gun after your scream, load
it, blast off in his boat to quiet the brute,
afterwards to visit your hospital bedside;
hippos can be ferocious, they do not scare
easily, gunshots merely scratch at their
eardrums and shells at their skins; thank
God your limbs are still together, man!

Thanksgiving

Lord, at fifty
you blessed him
with the fiery language
that smoked out demons
and their minions;

at sixty you let his
narratives rescue Grasmere
spiders drowning
in his bathtub;

in St George's at
seventy, you liquefied
his ice-numb limbs so
he could plod to the altar
for your holy host;

and now this
perfunctory garland,
Lord, what better
gift could crown
another life!

Now That They Have Brought Athena Down

Now that they have
brought Athena down
to her knees, split
the logs, clear the fire
place, gather the dry
twigs, make the fire,
sit the kids around
the lapping flames
and sing birdsongs
as the ancients did.

Sing of the hyena
who feasted himself
stupid everyday and
claimed he never saw
the latrine all his life
captivating listeners
as he stuffed himself
ever more and more;

Sing of the day hyena
abruptly felt himself
painfully clambering
the top of a local rock
nobody had ever dared,
there to squat and empty
his troubling rumbling
weary belly, then creep
back home as if planet
earth never happened;

Sing of the wrath of
the gods who, trailing
the stench that hyena
had deposited on their

sacred rock, marched
after him crying foul,
chanting about greed
and the folly of man.

Kalikalanje of *Ostrich Forest* *

CANTO I: *Birth*

'Kalikalanje, diminutive already
fried one; my name is Kalikalanje,

son of Kalanje and Likalanje, both
of Lanje, a village that has stood

by the woods of ancient *Ostrich
Forest* from the beginning of time.

How I came into the world, birth
elders amongst the Yao peoples of

Malawi, Mozambique, Tanzania,
wherever my tale is told by the fire,

have numerous varying accounts.
Some claim, 'Kalikalanje leapt out

of his mum's womb, of his own
accord and landed straight onto

her frying pan, there to turn him-
self over and over again until her

groundnut oil fried him clean and
dry.' Others attest, 'We pulled out

Kalikalanje from his mum's belly
and placed him on her pan to fry

---

* Translated and restructured into 12 cantos from a well-known legend of the
Yao peoples of Malawi, Mozambique and Tanzania.

clean and dry.' Yet others assert,
'We saw Kalikalanje kicking about

the grass and wattle beds of aged
Ostrich Forest, we picked him up

and restored him to his mum's glory
though later he jumped onto her pan

to fry clean and dry.' Some birth
elders dance before they declare,

'We *extracted* Kalikalanje, God's
diminutive already fried one, not

from his mum's womb, not from his
mum's belly, nor did we pick him

up from the grass and wattle beds of
Ostrich Forest, truly but truthfully

we *extorted* Kalikalanje from his
mum's knee, then he jumped onto

her pan to fry clean and dry.' Some
among such elders fiercely protest,

'No, we extracted Kalikalanje *not*
from his mum's knee, but from her

big toe, then we gave him liberty
to jump onto his mum's broiling

pan to fry clean and dry.' Others
contend, 'We *wrung* Kalikalanje

not from his mum's knee, not from
her big toe, but from her thumb;

he then leapt onto her pan to fry
clean and dry.' The accounts of

the tale of my birth, the birth of
Kalikalanje, God's already fried

diminutive, are legion; and if some
should acutely contradict others,

that's the spirit of my tale; the tale
of Kalikalanje, God's already fried

one; what birth elders and others
definitely agree on wherever they

tell my tale is: when I breathed my
first breath, at once I opened my

eyes and saw, at once I touched and
tasted, at once I heard and smelt,

at once I knew the past, the present,
the future; at once I began to talk,

think, imagine in my mum's tongue;
besides, at birth I did not scream as

foolish babies all over the world do;
after screaming with rapture at my

conception, I just thought it might be
prudent to merely chuckle at birth.'

CANTO II: *Free-range eggs*

The mystery of Kalikalanje began
early; when his mum was pregnant

with him, they had acute desire
for free-range eggs; Kalikalanje

whispered to his mum to get such
eggs deep down the woods where

homesteads fetched their firewood.
Indeed one morning she visited

ancient *Ostrich Forest* for firewood
when lo and behold colourful free-

range eggs lay before her, nested
for the picking; three free-range

eggs, as large as ostrich eggs, she
thought; she thanked her Creator,

gathered them onto her *chitenje*,
hurried home to prepare her meal;

but when she lifted the pestle as
she pounded her mix of millet, yam,

maize, rice, bananas in her mortar,
(the meal that would go with her

free-range eggs) a vulture-like bird
perched beside her. Kalikalanje's

mum jumped aside, pestle midair,
very visibly shaken, 'What kind

of visitation is this?' She greeted
her uninvited stranger. The bird

bullied her, 'No simple visitation
I fear, we saw them walking away

with our eggs just now, we came
to claim them back.' Kalikalanje

whispered for his mum to answer:
'Oh, that wasn't me but the urge

from here,' pointing at her big
belly. The bird stormed, 'Then

we'll have to chomp at mom and
her unborn or we demand our free-

range eggs back!' Kalikalanje's
mum cajoled, 'Why don't you wait

for his arrival just a few months
away, when you can have all of me,

all of him fresh, tender, delicious?'
First hesitation then concession,

'I suppose we should wait then!'
The bird mumbled and flew back

home fulminating that she had not
got what she had intended to get.

That night mum and unborn enjoyed
their meal with one free-range egg,

they saved the others for the future;
and for the next eight months, when

they needed free-range eggs, mum
simply visited ancient *Ostrich Forest*.

CANTO III: *Hatching*

One day, long after Kalikalanje's
birth, his mum was gathering

firewood in *Ostrich Forest* when
a voice behind her interrupted,

'I've got you today, thief of my
colourful free-range eggs! You

promised me your child; tell me
where I can find him or you die!'

It was the very same vulture that
demanded its colourful free-range

eggs years back. Kalikalanje's
mum inquired, 'Do you really

hatch free-range eggs?' The bird
challenged back, 'Colourful ones

I say, woman!' 'Then I know
the woman you really want; do

you see those houses over there?
That's where you'll find her; every-

one knows her; she boasts that
she's the only person who gets

colourful free-range eggs from the
woods of ancient *Ostrich Forest*;

whoever you meet will direct you
to her house; Likalanje's her name,

her husband's Kalanje, and he
went away some six years ago

with scores of men from villages
around here; as they declare, 'the

fellows were weary of our infinite
village bickering and paramount

chief's bother and tried to follow
their dreams', though with Kalanje

gone, Lanje had lost its best hunter
and best fisherman; and Kalanje

himself left his wife heavy with
child; the fellow did not even wait

for the birth of his baby as other
husbands would have done; and

when the baby arrived they called
it Kalikalanje, the already fried

one of Almighty.' The bird asked,
'When did this happen?' 'Oh, about

six years ago, why d'you ask, do you
know them?' 'Yes,' said the bird,

'I was invited to their son's birth
feast but was unable to go; anyway,

what are you doing in my forest?'
'What? You call this your forest?

But all God's people get their fire-
wood here, this is everybody's and

nobody's forest; anyway, let me
go; it's time to cook for my son.'

CANTO IV: *Bonded*

The bird flew towards Lanje village
and presently came across a squad

of boys playing ball; three bounced
their balls, one merely watched;

he had a quiver of arrows by his
side. 'Boys, stop!' the bird cried,

'Tell me which of these houses is
Likalanje's.' The boy with a quiver

of arrows by his side leapt forward
like a leader ready to defend his

gang, 'Tell us who you are first
and what your business is then

we'll answer you.' 'Lisimu, I am
Lisimu the awesome, the fearful;

when those ancient woods first
sprouted, I, Lisimu, already was;

Lisimu, power no one opposes or
clowns, Lisimu, the protector of

what you behold in ancient *Ostrich
Forest*, I mean everything therein!'

Thus the bird bragged on and
on until the boys fell apart with

laughter. Lisimu was incensed,
'Why d'you laugh so?' She tried

to scare them. 'It's your name; it's
the name of an ugly witch mums

sing about at story telling fires,'
boldly said the boy with a quiver

of arrows; he went on, 'Anyway,
you asked us, we'll answer you:

this is Likalanje's house; that
over there is Likalanje's; and the

house beside that is Likalanje's;
all the houses around here are

Likalanje's; which of them catches
your fancy?' Lisimu was suddenly

frozen, baffled; soon she headed
home furious that mere kids had

shamed the famed beast of *Ostrich
Forest* whom no one ever hassled.

CANTO V: *Birthday*

When Lisimu next met Likalanje
the former began, 'Hello! I know

everything about you now; one of
your friends told me your secrets;

your son arrived years ago; today
you won't get away, I demand my

colourful free-range eggs back or
you'll have to tell me where your

son hides, or you die!' Likalanje
was startled at first, then calmly

said, 'I've a plan; my son turns six
today and I've organised a party

for him, all his mates are coming
to celebrate with him; if you hide

behind this door, you will catch
him as he welcomes his mates;

everything I leave on this table is
theirs; the food, nibbles, drinks;

I am out visiting the neighbours next
door; they've come to settle here.'

But Kalikalanje welcomed his mates
outside the house saying: 'Let's

play our favourite game of masks
before the feast,' they all agreed

and transformed themselves into
cockroaches as they always did;

soon they began to nibble, nibble
at their food and sip at the drinks

as noiselessly as cockroaches can.
After unmasking themselves they

began to play football. Meanwhile,
Lisimu, who was dazed by the total

silence surrounding her hiding place,
peeped out and beheld to her shock

nothing, absolutely nobody before
her; the food, nibbles, drinks gone;

plates clear, bags of food, bottles
empty; she could hear kids playing

football nearby but daren't find
out; she merely slid out enraged.

CANTO VI: *Dance of monsters*

The following week Lisimu had
a gashing headache, she could

not recall the nightmares she'd
had that week; her struggle with

Likalanje and her son had spent
her time; she decided to kill them;

but first she'd appeal to the guild
of wizards, witches, snakes and

other noxious beasts of *Ostrich
Forest*. After days of persuasion,

coaxing, cowering, the beasts of
Ostrich Forest assembled under

nsolo tree where they made a fire;
carrying palm, reed, bamboo,

torches and banners they gathered
around their fire; presently low

voices of huge drums, sharp voices
of little drums mingled with light

tunes from the *mbira* of odd shapes
and sizes. Lisimu's ritual began;

the night tango of the monsters
of *Ostrich Forest* resounded noisy

and loud; the gadgets, amulets
that Lisimu was to wear on her

legs, ankles, wrists, waists as she
journeyed the woods of the world

were brought in; the fiends then
sprinkled dark medicinal waters

over Lisimu's body; they rubbed
her skin with herbal concoctions

that would blaze into submission
any thief of Lisimu's colourful free-

range eggs; she learnt how to
rub venom from mambas and

cobras of Malawi, Mozambique
and Tanzania mountain ranges

without poisoning herself as she
did so. After the ritual Lisimu

felt purified, utterly reassured;
she'd been exposed to the most

lethal herbs the woods of *Ostrich
Forest* ever prided in; in return

she vowed to offer the guild most
luscious chunks of flesh she'd get

from the men, women, kids who
stole her colourful free-range eggs;

but there was one major catch for
all these medicines to take effect:

Lisimu had to transmute herself,
abandon and renounce the masks

she preferred to wear when she
cruised the globe as these made

her the ugliest, most laughable
vulture known to *Ostrich Forest*.

CANTO VII: *Bundles of grass*

After many moons Lisimu visited
Lanje village determined to grab

whatever Likalanje owed for her
free-range eggs; this time she told

herself, 'I know their house and
have a special burden to execute

the pledge made with the guild
of the monsters of *Ostrich Forest*';

when Lisimu approached Likalanje,
however, the latter simply hushed

the former with: 'This time I have
a perfect plan which is foolproof;

my son will be getting bundles
of grass from the bush with his

mates; I'll hide you in one bundle;
when the boys come you'll judge for

yourself the best course of action.'
But Kalikalanje, who had brought

a gang of yelping, loud boys, stopped;
shushed his mates and bellowed at

the bundles of grass, 'Listen, where
I was born, when boys came to carry

home bundles of grass, they began
with bundles that kind of danced,

then each boy took home the bundle
of his choice!' Lisimu, who had left

no space in the bundle to see, could
not tell the speaker but took the cue

and made as if to dance, whereupon
Kalikalanje shocked, asked his mates,

'Guys, has anyone ever seen bundles
of grass dance, I suggest each grabs

his bundle save that one!' Lisimu
was left helpless, hapless, wretched.

CANTO VIII: *Fishy*

When Likalanje heard from Lisimu
what had happened, the former

goaded the latter, 'Lisimu, clever
as you are, why are you not able

to catch my son, Kalikalanje; are
you truly frightened of his mates?'

After a deep sigh Lisimu droned,
'Honestly, every time I am near

these kids some power freezes
me numb!' She did not submit

that the concoctions and charms
she wore were neutralised too. 'Is

that so?' Likalanje gibed, 'Okay
then, we will let him go fishing

in Milimbo waters; I'll shave one
side of his head for easy spotting;

when you see him you can simply
take him straight away, you hear?

Promise me you won't let him go
free this time!' But as the boys

returned home, their cords laden
with shiny fresh fish, Kalikalanje

helped his mates to shave one
side of their heads like him, 'lest

you-know-who should float about
menacing', he said. Indeed, frog-

veiled vulture came croaking,
'Fellows, which one among you

is called Kalikalanje, I bring
special messages for him only.'

Kalikalanje leapt forward with:
'This is Kalikalanje, that over

there is Kalikalanje, so is this
fellow beside me, I myself am

Kalikalanje as well; in truth,
we are all Kalikalanjes, which

of us deserves your messages?'
Lisimu stood frozen, the boys

screeched with glee fearless of
the beast they had recognised by

her little garbled voice. Infuriated,
Lisimu affirmed, 'I've had enough;

am done with this foolery; next
time I'll forget about this cunning

son and his naughty mates and
go straight for his mum; I have

to fulfill my pledge with the guild
of the beasts of *Ostrich Forest!*'

CANTO IX: *Honey*

Months after, Lisimu revisited
Likalanje; a quarrel erupted

about what Lisimu should do
next; transformed Kalikalanje

barged in to defend his mum;
their quarrel dropped; Lisimu

took Likalanje's offer: she'd send
her son with his mates to collect

honey in *Ostrich Forest*; Lisimu
was to trail and scatter the boys;

and as her son would be wearing
a red band on his wrist, Lisimu

would easily spot him. The gang
of boys arrived with dogs, bows,

arrows; two boys stood sentry
as Kalikalanje with two mates

extracted the honey from one
palm tree; the red band had been

multiplied, now each boy had
a red band on his wrist; Lisimu

could not tell who to go for; as
she was also frightened of dogs,

bows, arrows, she slipped away
and decided she'd not quarrel

with anyone any more; when they
met again she'd simply charge at

Likalanje, poke at her eyes, before
she knew it, she would be kicking

to death – she needed to fulfill
her pledge with the monsters.

When Lisimu revisited, Likalanje
whispered, 'Lisimu, quick, fly to

the rooftop, Kalikalanje will be
checking out the noises there any

minute now!' Before Kalikalanje
reached the rooftop, he shouted,

'Mum, it's dark here and a fiend
is squatting on the roof, pass me

dad's quiver of arrows!' On hearing
this Lisimu flew for her life. And

so Kalikalanje solemnly sat his
mum down and inquired, 'Mum,

this beast that wants to kill us,
what should we do about it?'

'I do not know what to do son,
we ate her colourful free-range

eggs and I love you,' she sobbed.
'Fine,' he said, 'I have an idea.'

CANTO X: *Returnees*

When Lanje village is happy all
surrounding villages are struck

by a celebratory bug too, they say;
the village headman who'd just

been enthroned as paramount chief,
replacing the one who had passed,

began his job by offering amnesty;
those who had left the villages

because they had quarrelled with
others, those who wanted to check

on the new paramount chief who
seemed more liberal, those who

were thrown out of exile for their
misdemeanour – they all returned

home one by one or in droves or
anyhow; clearly the animosities

that had raged among opposing
villages had abated; the land for

once enjoyed peace. The returnees
came back with many tales of joy,

terror and adventure; they also
brought home whatever they had

hoarded over the years, including
rugs, masks, beads, trinkets, what-

ever would cheer up their dances,
rituals, houses. Lanje was awash

with goods from returnees who'd
brought suits, dresses, trousers,

shorts, shirts, blankets, shoals,
shoes, soaps, perfumes, mirrors;

every family boasted new items
and almost every returnee who

went past the chief's house paid
homage to him with lots of gifts.

The chief was very pleased with
what he was offered and decreed

that there should be festivities
in order to honour the returnees;

cows, goats, sheep, chicken were
to be slaughtered; rice, bananas,

yam, millet, cassava, pumpkins
were to be cooked; fish of every

breed were to be cooked or fried;
okra, spinach, pumpkin leaves,

rape and other vegetables were
to be fried, cooked, boiled, some

in peanut butter. 'Let the drums
beat and rumble, let songs roar

across the land, let feasts happen
to honour returnees!' proclaimed

the paramount chief; happy gangs
of boys, girls gathered here, there,

everywhere, like the fortnight of
initiation ceremonies; the boys

who normally helped their elders
building reed, wattle or bamboo

grain storages or helped to mend
their fishing nets; the girls who

helped their mothers pound grain
or cook – they all left their chores

to rejoice at the returnees' festival;
Lanje village had never seen such

festivities; everyone was restive;
Kalikalanje was the most anxious;

his dad's return was so theatrical,
so spectacular, for, bearing a bronze

shield in one hand, a golden bow
slung over his shoulders, fishing

rods, penknives, a bunch of keys
clink-clanking about his waist,

he pushed his barrel of goods home
singing songs of victory, love; beer-

drinking, game-hunting songs too
sounded; then he offered his gifts.

CANTO XI: *My Dad*

Months after the returnees' feast,
dad invited mum and I to visit

the woods of *Ostrich Forest* with
him. 'I want to show you where

I used to hunt birds and game.'
On the way he apologised to mum

for going away while she was
pregnant when a good husband

should have waited on her and
left after I was born; mum took

his apology with a broad loving
smile; then dad recalled the feast

that the villages had mounted for
returnees; he joked about when

I would marry, what kind of girl
I fancied, from which community,

the cost of the wedding envisaged;
but mum was keen to inform dad

about the free-range eggs that she
once found in the woods. 'This is

where I saw the first set of eggs,'
she declared, 'I knew instantly

it was God who sent me here,
for, I found the eggs in neatly

ordered nests, as if some godly
powers had set them apart for

some pregnant woman like me;
and come, watch this!' she said.

Dad and I ran, 'Aaah,' dad said,
'What a beauty, how gorgeous;

have you two ever seen ostrich
eggs?' Dad asked. 'No,' mum

and I chorused. 'You have now,'
dad announced. 'So we thought,'

mum said, 'And were they tasty!'
she exclaimed. 'The only other bird

that could produce such stunning
eggs is the peacock, but I am sure

these are ostrich eggs,' dad said.
As we admired the colourful eggs,

the menacing vulture landed beside
us and utterly infuriated inquired,

'What are you three doing to my
eggs, do you want to steal these

as you did my colourful free-range
eggs years ago?' 'These are not

your eggs,' dad challenged her,
'How could an ugly vulture lay

striking eggs like these?' Their
voices echoed across the entire

forest; Lisimu was frozen stiff;
she'd never been openly opposed;

mum and I watched the match.
'Look, I've hunted these woods

as youth and adult, not once did
I hear the humbug that vultures

lay such special eggs, ostriches
or peacocks yes, but for vultures

to lay such eggs, tell me another
tale. Don't you recall that God

created the universe with people,
animals, birds, reptiles, crawling

creatures and placed them in this
forest; don't you recall ostriches

being fashioned flamboyant here –
hence the woods we call *Ostrich*

Forest?' dad bellowed with fury,
his voice booming everywhere;

then the dappled ostrich rudely
landed before us baying, 'What

in God's name are you four doing
to my eggs? So, it was you who

stole my eggs all the while?' 'No,'
interrupted mum, 'It was not all

of us; it was only me; when this
belly was full with him,' mum

was pointing at me, 'we had this
odd craving for free-range eggs;

as if God sent, I came here, saw
these eggs, took them home for

my son and me to eat; when he
arrived, the desire was gone, I

stopped gathering the eggs; but
this vulture has been claiming

that we ate her free-range eggs,
demanding that we return them

or else she'd kill my son and me!'
'You thief! So it's you who's been

stealing my eggs all the while, how
dare you claim my eggs are yours;

do we look alike? This mum and
son, are not guilty; their natural

craving brought them here; it's
you we must punish for stealing

my eggs and for threatening to
kill this mum and son who only

desired my eggs as they should;
you impostor, you liar, you worse

than hideous creature!' Verdict
having been thus pronounced, I,

Kalikalanje, God's diminutive
already fried one, son of Kalanje

and Likalanje, of Lanje village,
let loose dad's quiver of arrows.

CANTO XII: *Another tale*

Today, years on, no monument towers
to mark where Lanje village stood or

where I, Kalikalanje, the diminutive
already fried one of God, was born;

plaques to the woods of *Ostrich Forest*
are wiped clean and clear, the paths

that led to the nests where dappled
ostrich lay free-range eggs are beaten

dust dry; no one can guess vulture's
motives in her pursuit of what was

not hers, nor the encounters she had
with the monsters of *Ostrich Forest*

for her pledge not fulfilled; perhaps
another more tuneful narrative will be

fashioned to celebrate otherwise this
primeval tale for tomorrow's children.

NOTES

Now That They Have Brought Athena Down (51-52)

This is the song that the angry gods and the stinking mess together chanted as they followed hyena home to shame him before all.

a) *ja-mbitimbi ja-mbitimbi*
alitunu kulamba;
b) *ja-mbitimbi*
(x2)
a) *atiteje ngakunya*
b) *ja-mbitimbi*
a) *anyelele pesomwa,*
b) *ja-mbitimbi*
a) *aninde pelepo*
b) *ja-mbitimbi*
a) *aninde pelepo*
b) *ja-mbitimbi*

Kalikalanje of *Ostrich Forest* (53-78)

'Kalikalanje' is a well-known legend among the Yao-speaking peoples of Malawi, Mozambique and Tanzania. 'Kalikalanje' is a Yao word which refers to anyone who comes into the world endowed with knowledge of past, present, future times and events – hence the 'already fried one' title. Kalikalanje loves fun, freedom, peace, truth and justice; where any of these is absent he plays every trick available to achieve them. To some Kalikalanje is a menacing trickster who must be eliminated at all costs, although those who try only bring destruction upon themselves instead.

I am indebted to my mother who first told us (my sister, my brother and I) the story of Kalikalanje at the fireside. Some European missionary grammars of Yao record the legend too; *A Grammar of Yao Sentences* (OUP, 1966), based on Yao from Southern Tanzania and compiled by W.H. Whiteley, a distinguished Professor of Linguistics from London University is one. Professor Matthew Schoffeleers, the eminent anthropologist from the Netherlands, also gathered several versions of Kalikalanje, two of which appear in truncated forms in his and Adrian Roscoe's *Tales of Old Malawi* (Montfort Press, Malawi, 1985). And Professor Armindo Ngunga of Eduardo Mondlane University, Mozambique, remembers a version of Kalikalanje from his childhood. Recently Mrs Joyce Jaffu offered me more versions of Kalikalanje from Mangochi district, Malawi.

Obviously my debt to these versions is enormous and I must concede that in translation the original Yao idiophones, grammatical and sentential structures have been sacrificed in favour of clarity. But I hope to have retained, augmented, perhaps even enriched the tale's symbolic, social-cultural-political nuance that is relevant in today's world of persistent liars and impostors.